W9-BAI-389

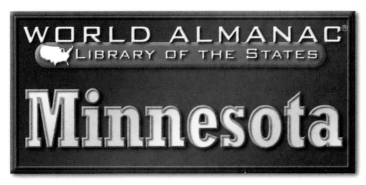

LAND OF 10,000 LAKES

by Miriam Heddy Pollock and Peter Jaffe

Curriculum Consultant: Jean Craven,
Director of Instructional Support,
Albuquerque, NM, Public Schools

WORLD ALMANAC® LIBRARY

Please visit our web site at: **www.worldalmanaclibrary.com**
For a free color catalog describing World Almanac® Library's
list of high-quality books and multimedia programs, call
1-800-848-2928 (USA) or 1-800-387-3178 (Canada).
World Almanac® Library's fax: (414) 332-3567.

Library of Congress Cataloging-in-Publication Data

Pollock, Miriam Heddy.
    Minnesota, Land of 10,000 Lakes / by Miriam Heddy Pollock and Peter Jaffe.
        p. cm. — (World Almanac Library of the states)
    Includes bibliographical references and index.
    Summary: Illustrations and text present the history, geography, people, politics and
government, economy, and social life and customs of Minnesota, which is also known
as "The North Star State."
    ISBN 0-8368-5138-2 (lib. bdg.)
    ISBN 0-8368-5308-3 (softcover)
    1. Minnesota—Juvenile literature. [1. Minnesota.] I. Title: Minnesota. II. Jaffe,
Peter. III. Title. IV. Series.
    F606.3.P65   2002
    977.6—dc21   2002022707

This edition first published in 2002 by
World Almanac® Library
330 West Olive Street, Suite 100
Milwaukee, WI 53212 USA

This edition © 2002 by World Almanac® Library.

Design and Editorial: Bill SMITH STUDIO Inc.
Editor: Kristen Behrens
Assistant Editor: Megan Elias
Art Director: Jay Jaffe
Photo Research: Sean Livingstone
Production: Maureen O'Connor
World Almanac® Library Project Editor: Patricia Lantier
World Almanac® Library Editors: Catherine Gardner, Monica Rausch
World Almanac® Library Production: Scott M. Krall, Tammy Gruenewald,
  Katherine A. Goedheer

Photo credits: p.4-5 © PhotoDisc; p.6 (bottom left) © Corel; (top right) © Corel; (bottom right)
© PhotoDisc; p. 7 (top) courtesy Mars Inc.; (bottom) © Corel; p.9 © ArtToday; p.10 © Minnesota
Historical Society/CORBIS; p.11 © Library of Congress; p.12 © Dover; p.13 © Corbis; p.14
© Library of Congress; p.15 © PhotoDisc; p.17 © Gordon Coster/TimePix; p.18 © PhotoDisc;
p.20 (left to right) © Corel; © Painet; © Painet; p.21 (left to right) © Painet; © PhotoDisc;
© Corel; p.23 © Corel; p.26 (inset) © PhotoDisc; (bottom) © Library of Congress; p.27 ©
PhotoDisc; p.29 © Keri Pickett/TimePix; p.31 © PhotoDisc; p.32 © PhotoDisc; p.33 (top) Duluth
CVB; (inset) © Corel; p.34 courtesy of Prairie Home Companion; p.35 © Eric Miller/TimePix;
p.36 courtesy of the St. Paul CVB; p.37 © Richard Cummins/CORBIS; p.38 © PhotoDisc; p.39
© ArtToday; p.40 © John Burgess/Santa Rosa Press-Democrat/Liason; p.41 (top) © Gary
Hershorn/TimePix; (bottom) © PhotoDisc; p.42-43 © Library of Congress; p.44 (top) © PhotoDisc;
(bottom) © PhotoSpin; p.45 (top) © PhotoDisc; (bottom) © Corel

Printed in the United States of America

1 2 3 4 5 6 7 8 9 06 05 04 03 02

Minnesota

Northern Star

It is appropriate that Minnesota's motto is *L'Etoile du Nord*, or "The Star of the North," because it is the northernmost of the "lower 48" states. Minnesota is also known as the Land of 10,000 Lakes. Thanks to these lakes and more than five thousand rivers and streams, water sports are among the state's most popular pastimes. Legend has it that the giant lumberjack Paul Bunyan and Babe, his blue ox, created all these lakes as they walked over the state and their mighty footprints filled with rainwater. Paul Bunyan himself is closely associated with the timberland of the northeastern part of the state.

Perhaps the most distinctive feature in the state is the mighty Mississippi River, which has its headwaters in Lake Itasca in northern Minnesota. The river divides the Twin Cities of Minneapolis and St. Paul, the two largest urban areas in Minnesota. For many years there was a rivalry between the two since St. Paul was the state capital, yet Minneapolis had a larger population — each city wanted what the other one had. In modern times, however, the Twin Cities act more like good siblings, sharing a common culture and a vast suburban area.

Today Minnesota has a diverse economy, with a large agricultural base, high-tech industries, and profitable use of its natural resources. The state started out as a haven for hunters and trappers, who exploited the lakes and streams as sources of animals and as ways to transport pelts out of the region. Logging and mining have helped shape the state's economy, but they have also caused some environmental problems. With the start of the twenty-first century, however, the state is working to use its resources while preserving its natural beauty.

▶ Map of Minnesota showing the interstate highway system, as well as major cities and waterways.

▼ A steamboat on the Mississippi River, which is Minnesota's major waterway.

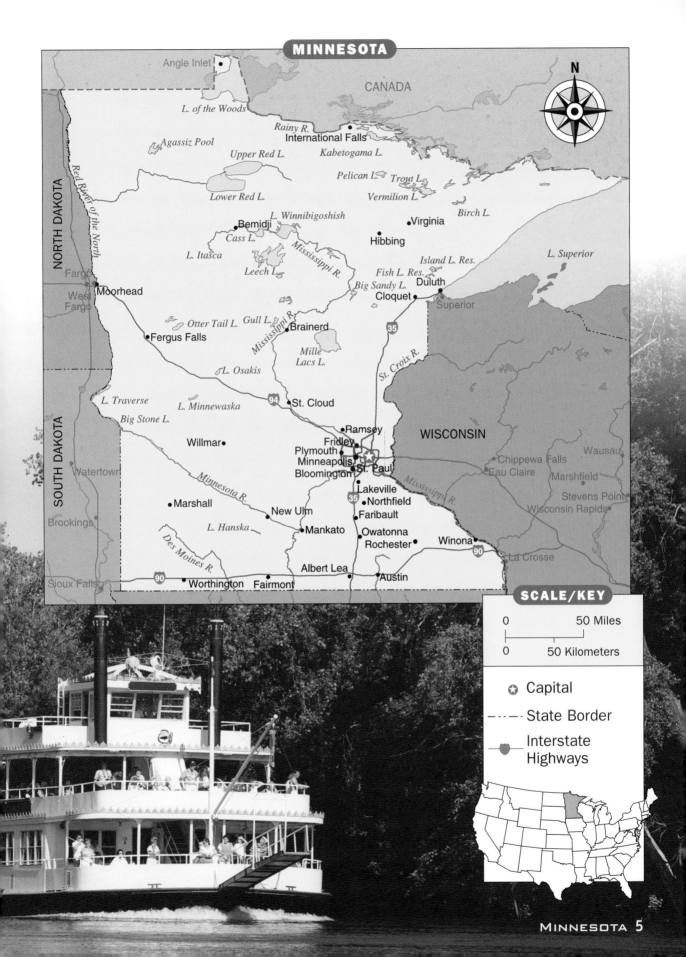

MINNESOTA

CANADA

N

Angle Inlet

L. of the Woods

Rainy R.
International Falls

Agassiz Pool

Upper Red L.

Kabetogama L.

Pelican L. Trout L.

Vermilion L.

Birch L.

Lower Red L.

Bemidji L. Winnibigoshish

Virginia

Cass L.

Hibbing

L. Itasca

Mississippi R.

Island L. Res.

L. Superior

Leech L.

Fish L. Res.
Big Sandy L. Duluth

NORTH DAKOTA

Red River of the North

Fargo

West Fargo

Moorhead

Cloquet

Superior

Otter Tail L. Gull L.

Mississippi R.

Brainerd

35

Fergus Falls

Mille
Lacs L.

St. Croix R.

L. Osakis

WISCONSIN

L. Traverse

L. Minnewaska

94

St. Cloud

Big Stone L.

Watertown

SOUTH DAKOTA

Willmar

Ramsey

Fridley
Plymouth
Minneapolis
Bloomington

St. Paul

Chippewa Falls Wausau

Eau Claire Marshfield

Minnesota R.

Lakeville

35

Mississippi R.

Stevens Point
Wisconsin Rapids

Marshall

Northfield
Faribault

Brookings

L. Hanska

New Ulm

Mankato

Owatonna
Rochester

Winona

90

La Crosse

Des Moines R.

Albert Lea

Austin

Sioux Falls

90

Worthington Fairmont

Fast Facts

MINNESOTA (MN), Land of 10,000 Lakes

Entered Union

May 11, 1858 (32nd state)

Capital	Population
St. Paul	287,151

Total Population (2000)

4,919,479 (21st most populous state) — *Between 1990 and 2000, population of Minnesota increased by 12.4 percent.*

Largest Cities	Population
Minneapolis	382,618
St. Paul	287,151
Duluth	86,918
Rochester	85,806
Bloomington	85,172

Land Area

79,610 square miles (206,190 square kilometers) (14th largest state)

State Motto

L'Etoile du Nord — *French for "The Star of the North." Minnesota is also known as the North Star State.*

State Song

"Hail! Minnesota" by Truman E. Rickard and Arthur E. Upson, adopted in 1945.

State Bird

Common loon — *The word* loon *comes from a Norwegian word meaning "wild, sad cry." Loons have a distinctive mournful call. Loons are one of Earth's oldest bird species — about sixty million years old.*

State Fish

Walleye pike

State Butterfly

Monarch — *This insect is also sometimes called the milkweed butterfly.*

State Tree

Norway or red pine — *The tallest Norway pine in Minnesota stands in Itasca State Park. It is 120 feet (37 meters) high and more than three hundred years old.*

State Flower

Pink-and-white lady's slipper — *This slow-growing plant can take as long as four to sixteen years to produce its first flower.*

State Mushroom

Morel

State Grain

Wild rice — *This grain grows in the shallow waters of the lakes of central and northern Minnesota. Native American tribes are granted the right to the first harvest.*

State Muffin

Blueberry — *This fruit, one of the three cultivated fruits native to North America, grows in the wild throughout northeastern Minnesota.*

PLACES TO VISIT

Pipestone National Monument, *Pipestone*
As many as two thousand years ago, people who lived on the Plains used the rock mined in quarries here to create sacred pipes, more commonly called peace pipes. By the 1700s the Dakota (also called Sioux) were trading the rock they quarried with other tribes. By 1937 the quarries were designated a National Monument.

Science Museum of Minnesota, *St. Paul*
Use a musical stairway to travel from the dinosaur display to Experimental Gallery, or watch a movie projected by the world's largest film projector. The museum also includes the Questionable Medical Devices Collection.

Voyageurs National Park, *near International Falls*
Named for the French *voyageurs,* or fur traders, this national park has thirty lakes and unparalleled fishing — even ice fishing in the wintertime. Wildlife abounds, including eagles, beavers, otters, moose, and wolves.

For other places and events, see p. 44.

BIGGEST, BEST, AND MOST

- Minnesota has more recreational boats per person than any other state — one boat for every six people.

- The largest enclosed shopping mall in the United States is the Mall of America, located in Bloomington.

STATE FIRSTS

- **1919** Minnesotan Charles Strite invents the first pop-up electric toaster. The toaster was just one of the many innovative products created in the state. Others include water skis (1922), Scotch tape (1930), the supercomputer (1963), and Post-it Notes (1980).

- **1933** The first sit-down strike in the United States is held at the packing plant of George A. Hormel and Company in Austin.

Out of This World

In 1923 a beloved candy bar was born. Candy maker Frank C. Mars of Minneapolis layered chocolate-malt flavored nougat and caramel, then coated the layers in chocolate. When the resulting "Milky Way" bar arrived in stores, it was an instant hit. Mars followed up on his initial success by adding peanuts to the mix, creating Snickers in 1930. In 1932 he introduced 3 Musketeers. Originally, 3 Musketeers were sold three to a package, and each bar was filled with one of three different flavors of nougat.

High Lonesome Sound

Early settlers in Minnesota feared the native timber wolves, and efforts were made to eliminate wolves from the landscape. The state government paid a bounty on wolf pelts. In 1849 each pelt was worth $3, and by 1965 that amount had risen to $35. The state's policy toward wolves changed in 1974, however, when timber wolves were placed on the endangered species list. Since that time Minnesota has worked to protect the wolves and restore their population. These efforts have succeeded. Today Minnesota's timber wolf population stands at more than sixteen hundred.

From Northwest to Midwest

My present residence is on the utmost verge of civilization in the northwestern part of the United States, within a few miles of the principal village of white men in the territory that we suppose will bear the name of Minnesota, which some would render, 'clear water,' though strictly, it signifies slightly turbid or whitish water.

— *Rev. Dr. Williamson (of the Sioux Mission) quoted in Harriet E. Bishop's* Floral Home; or, First Years of Minnesota, *1857*

Archaeological records suggest that there have been people in what is now Minnesota since the last ice age, as many as ten thousand years ago. In fact, some skeletons have been found that may be more than twenty-five thousand years old. The earliest inhabitants were nomadic hunters who came to the region in pursuit of large animals, such as mammoths.

As the glaciers receded, people slowly — over thousands of years — began to develop methods of cultivating crops, rather than just hunting and gathering food in the wild. It was not until about three thousand years ago that people began to develop more permanent settlements. Mound Builders, so called because ceremonial mounds were an important part of their culture, occupied much of what is now the midwestern United States. Minnesota was at the edge of territory inhabited by the Hopewell, a culture that was prevalent in what are now Ohio and Illinois. The Hopewell people left behind thousands of mounds.

About one thousand years ago, people of the Mississippian culture began arriving in the area, traveling north up the Mississippi River. The Mississippians brought along aspects of their southern culture and influenced the Mound Builders. For a time the Oto, Omaha, and Iowa occupied southern present-day Minnesota. By the time Europeans began to arrive in the seventeenth century, however, the region was occupied by the Dakota, also known as the Sioux. They had been in the region for many years, and their culture bore vestiges of the Mississippians who had come before.

Native Americans of Minnesota

Anishinabe (Ojibwa, Chippewa)
Dakota (Sioux)
Hopewell
Iowa
Omaha
Oto

DID YOU KNOW?

The name *Minnesota* comes from the Dakota word *minisota*, meaning "water that reflects the sky" or "sky-tinted water."

In the late sixteenth century, the Anishinabe (sometimes called Ojibwa or Chippewa) tribe moved in from the east. The Anishinabe quickly gained territory as they traded with European explorers for weapons and other items that gave them advantages over their neighbors. The Anishinabe drove the Dakota out of the northern part of the state, gaining control by the end of the eighteenth century.

Exploration and Colonization

Although Vikings were rumored to have visited Minnesota in the fourteenth century, most historians now consider the Viking artifacts found in 1898 near the town of Kensington to be a hoax. The first verifiable European arrival in Minnesota was in the mid-seventeenth century. French traders Médard Chouart, Sieur des Groseilliers, and Pierre Esprit Radisson explored the western end of Lake Superior in 1659, establishing France's claim to the region. They then spent the winter with the Dakota in the Mille Lacs region. *Mille Lacs* is French for "one thousand lakes." Other Europeans who came to the region soon after were also from France. In 1673 Father Jacques Marquette and Louis Jolliet explored the upper part of the Mississippi River. In 1680, Father Louis Hennepin also began to explore the

DID YOU KNOW?

Many European and U.S. explorers searched for the source of the Mississippi River, and some thought they had found it. Many historians believe it was not until 1832 that Henry Rowe Schoolcraft, assisted by an Anishinabe named Ozawindib, located the true source of the river and named it Lake Itasca.

▼ Father Jacques Marquette preached to Native Americans in their own language.

Father Louis Hennepin

The man for whom Hennepin County (home to Minneapolis) is named was a Franciscan friar who first came to the region with French explorer Robert Cavalier, Sieur de La Salle, as chaplain to the explorer's Western expedition. La Salle and Hennepin reached Illinois in 1680 and established Fort Crèvecoeur at the modern site of Peoria. La Salle sent Father Hennepin with a party exploring the northern reaches of the Mississippi River while he returned east for supplies. However, in April 1680 the explorers were captured by a group of Dakota and held for several months. While they were held captive, the explorers accompanied the Dakota on hunting expeditions. During one of these Father Hennepin observed and named the Falls of St. Anthony, the spot on the Mississippi where Minneapolis would one day be founded. When he was rescued by the French explorer Daniel Greysolon, Sieur Dulhut (or Duluth), in July, Father Hennepin traveled back to his native France, where he wrote the first book describing the northern Mississippi, *Description de la Louisiane* (1683). A later revision of the book was titled *A New Discovery of a Vast Country in America* (1698).

region. Pierre Charles Le Sueur built a trading post on Prairie Island (in the Mississippi River) as early as 1695 and in 1700 built a fort near present-day Mankato.

The European influx continued throughout the eighteenth century, consisting primarily of French traders and explorers. By mid-century, however, the French drive to colonize the Americas was waning. In 1762 France gave Spain land that included the part of Minnesota that is west of the Mississippi. The following year control of the eastern part of the region was given to Great Britain in the Treaty of Paris, which concluded the French and Indian War. That war was part of a larger European conflict known as the Seven Years' War (1756–1763).

After the Revolutionary War, the British holdings passed to the United States. The eastern area became part of the Northwest Territory with the Ordinance of 1787. In 1800 the western half of the area was returned to French control, but with the Louisiana Purchase of 1803, the western regions of what would become Minnesota were sold to the United States. The British, however, maintained a presence in the northwestern regions.

When the War of 1812 broke out over U.S. resentment of the British Navy's restrictive control of the Atlantic Ocean, the northwest region of present-day Minnesota became a frequent battleground. In many cases the British encouraged Native Americans to attack the United States. When the war ended, Britain finally withdrew from the northwest. The U.S. Army began to establish posts in Minnesota as early as 1819.

Territory and State

Minnesota, or some part of it, was included in several other U.S. territories before finally becoming a territory itself. In 1818 the Michigan Territory was extended to the Mississippi River, encompassing the eastern half of Minnesota. In 1836 the Wisconsin Territory was established, which included all of what would eventually be Minnesota. Two years later, however, the newly formed Iowa Territory claimed the part of Minnesota west of the Mississippi. In 1849 the Minnesota Territory was finally established, with Alexander Ramsey as governor. Slavery was prohibited and free public education was provided for by law.

Two years later Ramsey helped negotiate a treaty between the eastern Dakota nation and the U.S. government — the Treaty of Traverse des Sioux — in which most of the Dakota land in Minnesota was relinquished to the United States. In return for giving up their land, the Dakota were promised food and other necessities, as well as schooling and cash payments. The bulk of the money was set aside in a trust, to be paid out in annual installments. After the treaty was negotiated, however, the U.S. government used most of the trust money to pay off its own debts. The Dakota received only a small fraction of the promised money, with much of the rest going to white traders from whom the Dakota had supposedly made purchases on credit. The other resources promised were never fully delivered. The result was a growing resentment by the Dakota against the settlers in Minnesota.

Pike's Treaties

One of the earliest treaties signed between the U.S. government and the Dakota came in 1805. Zebulon Pike was assigned by Thomas Jefferson to lead an expedition exploring north-central Minnesota, and he traveled as far as Leech Lake. As part of the expedition, Pike was also to establish military posts. He negotiated with the Dakota for a parcel of land measuring 9 square miles (23 sq km) at the mouth of the St. Croix River and another at the point where the Mississippi and Minnesota Rivers meet (the modern site of the Twin Cities).

◀ U.S. artist Frank Blackwell Mayer made these sketches of camp life on the Traverse des Sioux in 1851. Mayer was well-known for his portraits of Native American and pioneer life.

In 1857 a state constitutional convention was held, and a constitution was drafted successfully. The voters approved it almost unanimously three months later. Minnesota became the thirty-second state on May 11, 1858. Henry Hastings Sibley became the new state's first governor. He was succeeded two years later by former territorial governor Alexander Ramsey.

The population grew rapidly throughout the 1850s. Much of the state was fertile farmland, and, after the Treaty of Traverse des Sioux was signed in 1851, settlers began pouring in. Easy access to the southern states and the Gulf of Mexico (via the Mississippi) and to the East Coast (via the Great Lakes and St. Lawrence River) made large-scale farming lucrative. Wheat became a major crop and one of the state's greatest exports. Lumber likewise became an important industry due to the vast forests as well as the ease of transporting logs through the state's waterways. At the start of the decade, there were approximately six thousand non-Natives living in Minnesota, in addition to Native Americans. By 1860 the total population had grown to more than 170,000. About one-third of that number were immigrants from overseas.

The Civil War and the Dakota Conflict

When the Civil War began in 1861, Minnesota governor Alexander Ramsey was in Washington, D.C. Word of the Confederate attack on South Carolina's Fort Sumter reached the nation's capital on the evening of April 13. The next morning, Ramsey rushed to the Secretary of War and pledged one thousand troops, making Minnesota the first state to offer soldiers to aid the Union effort in the war.

Initially the state was not prepared to fulfill such an offer. Although the state militia was supposed to consist of twenty-six thousand men, it actually numbered only a few hundred active troops. When the call went out for volunteers, however, there was no shortage. By April 30 the First Minnesota Volunteer Infantry had been organized, and, although most volunteers had little or no military training, the company numbered more than nine hundred men. Thousands more were to follow. While there were

Chief Little Crow

The leader of the Dakota uprising of 1862 was named Taoyateduta ("His Red Nation") but was called in English "Little Crow." He became the leader of the Kaposia Dakota tribe in 1846, succeeding his father, Charging Hawk, who died of an accidental gunshot wound. It was a time when his people were being forced from their traditional lands, piece by piece. They were promised much but given little in return. Many within the tribe argued for war with the white settlers. Although Little Crow opposed this war, believing it impossible to win, he knew his people would not be appeased and was forced to lead them in a lost cause. When the war turned out disastrously for the Dakota, Little Crow was discredited.

plenty of volunteers ready to serve in the Union Army, supplies were extremely short. There was hardly enough food to distribute to the soldiers, they had no regular uniforms, and high-quality weapons were not available.

On July 21 at the First Battle of Bull Run, the First Minnesota regiment fought bravely. They refused to retreat until ordered to do so for a third time, and lost more men than any other Union regiment at that battle. Minnesota fighters continued to distinguish themselves throughout the war.

Meanwhile trouble was brewing among the Dakota people. Many Dakota resented losing their tribal lands in the treaties signed ten years before, and Dakota leaders were concerned that contact with the settlers was weakening tribal traditions. The Dakota believed the U.S. government was not living up to its promise to supply money and food. The Treaty of Traverse des Sioux was worthless to the Dakota.

By 1862 the Dakota had been placed on a small reservation on the banks of the Minnesota River. Conditions were bad, and the Dakota felt they had been betrayed by the United States. In frustration four Dakota

▼ On July 21, 1861, the First Minnesota regiment joined other Union troops in an unsuccessful assault against Confederate forces at the First Battle of Bull Run.

men killed five white settlers who were living on land that had previously belonged to the Dakota. After the attack the Dakota men returned to their reservation and the tribe met to discuss a strategy. Many favored waging war against the United States.

Little Crow, a Dakota chief, led a group of warriors to the Redwood Agency near the reservation, where they killed approximately twenty men. This battle was the beginning of an uprising that lasted for more than a month. As the Dakota attempted to reassert their ownership of the land, the settlers resisted. Henry Sibley led the military units that defended the settlements. The Dakota killed more than four hundred people during their rebellion and took more than two hundred prisoners. In late September at Yellow Medicine, Little Crow and his warriors were no longer able to hold off Sibley and his men. Little Crow retreated to the north, but the Dakota who stayed behind were punished severely by the U.S. government. Over a period of six weeks, a U.S. military court tried nearly four hundred people, convicting more than three hundred of them. Thirty-eight were hanged in the largest mass execution in the nation's history.

Boom Times

Minnesota grew rapidly in the years following the Civil War. The population reached nearly 440,000 by 1870 and was more than 780,000 by 1880. During the 1880s the state experienced its most intense period of growth. This was the decade in which the logging industry was at its peak; iron ore was discovered in the northeastern part of the state; and the western part of the state experienced a rush of settlers. Wheat became an even more important component

The Minnesota Fighting Spirit

The Motor Corps Company of Minnesota, shown above, was just a small part of Minnesota's contribution to World War I. Minnesota has always sent its share of troops in times of war. Minnesota was the first state to volunteer troops to the Union army in the Civil War. More than 120,000 Minnesotans served in World War I, more than 300,000 in World War II, and 137,000 in the Korean War. Nearly 70,000 Minnesotans served in the Vietnam War and more than 11,000 in the Persian Gulf War.

of the state's economy after lumber and flour mills were built to harness the power of St. Anthony Falls.

In 1900 more than 1.75 million people lived in the state. By the time of the Great Depression in 1929, the population had reached 2.5 million. Although some states were hit harder, many Minnesotans lost their jobs during the Great Depression when businesses went bankrupt and demand declined for the state's main exports of lumber and wheat.

Modern Minnesota

After World War II a shift began in the state's economy. Agriculture and the environmentally damaging industries of logging and mining declined in importance, and a new emphasis on technology appeared. In 1948, for the first time, the state produced more goods through manufacturing than agriculture. Reflecting a national trend, the economy has recently shifted more and more toward the service industries and high-tech manufacturing.

Meanwhile the population has continued to grow. There are now almost five million people living in Minnesota. Although only 4 percent still work on farms, nearly one-third live in rural areas.

▼ After World War II, Minnesota's economy shifted toward industry and manufacturing. Ports like Duluth, on the Great Lakes, became vital to the state's future.

Vikings, Miners, and Lumberjacks

> Minnesota, a prairie country, rolling, but with no important hills, well watered, well grassed, with a repellant reputation for severe winters, not well adapted to corn, nor friendly to most fruits, attracted nevertheless hardy and adventurous people, and proved specially inviting to the Scandinavians, who are tough and industrious.
> — *Charles Dudley Warner*, Studies in the South and West, *1889*

The 2000 U.S. Census recorded almost five million people living in Minnesota, an increase of more than 12 percent from 1990. This puts the state just slightly ahead of the U.S. mean, as the twenty-first most populous state. Much of the state is woodland and farmland, and about 30 percent of Minnesotans live in rural areas. People in Minnesota are generally well educated: 89.5 percent of adults twenty-five years and older have high school diplomas, while 28 percent have at least a bachelor's degree. The median age in Minnesota is 35.4 years, just slightly higher than the national median of 35.3 years. Among adults there are 5 percent more women than men in Minnesota.

Age Distribution in Minnesota (2000 Census)	
0–4	329,594
5–19	1,105,251
20–24	322,483
25–44	1,497,320
45–64	1,070,565
65 & over	594,266

Across One Hundred Years

Minnesota's three largest foreign-born groups for 1890 and 1990

1890 | 1990

Germany	Norway	Sweden
116,955	101,169	99,913

Total state population: 1,301,826
Total foreign-born: 467,356 (36%)

Laos	Canada	Vietnam
14,979	10,339	7,772

Total state population: 4,375,099
Total foreign-born: 113,039 (3%)

Patterns of Immigration

The total number of people who immigrated to Minnesota in 1998 was 6,981. Of that number the largest immigrant groups were from Mexico (7.7%), India (6.5%), and Vietnam (4.7%).

The Viking State?

Although Minnesota is famous for its Scandinavian population and supposed discovery by Vikings, there are actually far more people of German descent than of any other ancestry. More than 1.8 million Minnesotans, or 37 percent of the population, are descended from German immigrants. People of Norwegian ancestry account for 16 percent of the population, and rounding out the top five are the Irish with 11 percent, Swedish with 9 percent, and English with 7 percent. The total Scandinavian population is more than 25 percent, however, so that region's contributions to the state are still important. All in all, almost 90 percent of the population is white, according to the 2000 Census.

▲ A group of farmers in East Grand Forks in 1943 enjoys lunch while pausing briefly during a wheat harvest.

Immigration

Although the population is primarily descended from people who immigrated in the nineteenth century, not many people move to Minnesota from overseas today. As of 2000 about 5 percent of the population is foreign-born. One group that has immigrated to Minnesota in recent years is the Hmong

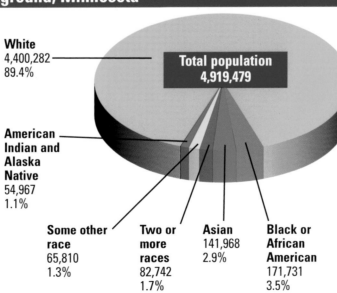

Heritage and Background, Minnesota — Year 2000

▶ Here's a look at the racial backgrounds of Minnesotans today. Minnesota ranks thirty-seventh among all U.S. states with regard to African Americans as a percentage of the population.

Total population 4,919,479

White
4,400,282
89.4%

American Indian and Alaska Native
54,967
1.1%

Native Hawaiian and other Pacific Islander
1,979
0.1%

Some other race
65,810
1.3%

Two or more races
82,742
1.7%

Asian
141,968
2.9%

Black or African American
171,731
3.5%

Note: 2.9% (143,382) of the population identify themselves as **Hispanic** or **Latino,** a cultural designation that crosses racial lines. Hispanics and Latinos are counted in this category as well as the racial category of their choice.

people of Laos. After the United States withdrew from the Vietnam War in the 1970s, thousands of Hmong, who had aided the United States during the war, were forced to flee their homes. The U.S. government helped relocate them, and tens of thousands of Hmong settled in St. Paul. The Twin Cities are now believed to have the largest concentration of Hmong people in the United States.

Big Cities

By far the most densely populated part of Minnesota is the Twin Cities metropolitan area, with approximately

Educational Levels of Minnesota Workers (age 25 and over)	
Less than 9th grade	130,140
9th to 12th grade, no diploma	194,266
High school graduate, including equivalency	950,942
Some college, no degree or associate degree	717,496
Bachelor's degree	594,980
Graduate or professional degree	265,493

▼ The skyscrapers of Minneapolis look out on the wooded plains of the state.

three million residents — more than half the state's total population. St. Paul was founded in 1838 on the east bank of the Mississippi. Minneapolis was chartered in 1867 on the west bank. Minneapolis grew up near the town of St. Anthony, which was an established village in the 1840s. In 1872 St. Anthony and Minneapolis became one city. For many years Minneapolis and St. Paul vied to be the largest and most important city in the state. As the capital, St. Paul had the upper hand, but Minneapolis eventually overtook its neighbor in population. Today the cities have a friendly relationship. This is due in part to the fact that most of the area's population now lives in suburbs outside either city and in part because the cities now share a vibrant cultural life.

Education

Minnesota has a good public school system, as is shown by the high (nearly 90 percent) graduation rate — the fourth-highest in the nation. About 90 percent of school-aged children in Minnesota attend public schools. The drive to have a well-educated populace goes back to the state constitution, which calls for free primary education for all people below the age of twenty-three. Today the state still offers some students the opportunity to attend college free of tuition.

The University of Minnesota was created in 1851. It closed during the Civil War and reopened in 1869. The university is made up of forty-four colleges that enroll a combined total of more than sixty thousand students. The state is also home to seven other state universities, twenty-six private liberal arts colleges, seventeen private graduate schools, and twenty-nine community and technical colleges.

Religion

Many religions are observed in Minnesota. The majority of Minnesotans, however — almost 90 percent — are Christian. No other religion accounts for even 1 percent of the total population — 0.8 percent are Jewish; 0.6 percent are agnostic; and 0.4 percent are Unitarian. Buddhists, Hindus, and Muslims each make up 0.1 percent of Minnesota's population. Another 0.8 percent practice other religions, although no single religion in this group makes up even one-tenth of 1 percent of the population.

Land of Lakes and Forests

> The Navigation of the Meschasipi is interrupted ten Leagues above this River of the Grave, by a Fall of fifty or sixty Foot, which we call'd The Fall of St. Anthony of Padua, whom we had taken for the Protector of our Discovery. There is a Rock of a Pyramidal Figure, just in the middle of the Fall of the River.
>
> — *Father Louis Hennepin*, A New Discovery of a Vast Country in America … between New France and New Mexico, *1698*

Minnesota has a land area of 79,610 square miles (206,190 sq km), making it the fourteenth largest state. It is as much as 350 miles (563 km) long from north to south and 357 miles (574 km) wide at the northern border. Because the eastern border of the state curves inward, the average width of the state is only 206 miles (332 km). Minnesota shares borders with four other states: North Dakota and South Dakota to the west, Iowa to the south, and Wisconsin to the east. To the north are the Canadian provinces of Manitoba and Ontario.

Climate

Minnesota includes the northernmost point among the "lower 48" states — Angle Inlet, a community north of the forty-ninth parallel. Because the state is so long, and its northern border is so far north, Minnesota often seems to be experiencing two seasons at once. Spring comes to the

Highest Point

Eagle Mountain
2,301 feet (701 m)
above sea level

▼ *From left to right:* A Minnesota cornfield; a forest in autumn; Lake Superior; a winter scene; Minneapolis–St. Paul; a Minnesotan moose.

southern part of the state a month before it arrives in the north. The average temperature in July is 68°F (20°C) in the north and 74°F (23°C) in the south, the ninth lowest high among U.S. states. The average in January is a chilly 2°F (-17°C) in the north, one of the coldest lows in the United States, and 15°F (-9°C) in the south. The weather gets so cold in the winter, and stays cold for so long, that parts of some cities, such as Minneapolis, are connected by tubes or underground passages so that people don't have to venture outside.

Lakes and Rivers

Minnesota is known as the "Land of 10,000 Lakes," but in reality, there are more than 15,000 lakes, 12,000 of which are more than 10 acres (4 ha) in size. Many of the lakes were formed when glaciers carved up the land and then retreated about eight thousand years ago. The largest lakes entirely within the state's borders are Upper Red Lake (288,800 acres / 116,877 ha) and Mille Lacs Lake (132,516 acres / 53,629 ha). Excluding Lake Superior, which shapes the northeastern corner of the state, there are more than 4,700 square miles (12,173 sq km) of water in Minnesota, the third greatest amount of water area in the nation.

The more than 6,500 rivers and streams have a combined length of 92,000 miles (148,028 km). The most important river is the Mississippi, which begins in Lake Itasca in north-central Minnesota and flows all the way to the Gulf of Mexico. Other major rivers include the Minnesota and the Red River of the North, which marks the North Dakota border. The Minnesota River was named *minisota* by the Dakota people. The name means "water that reflects the sky" or "sky-tinted water," and it is easy to see why this name was chosen for the state.

Average January temperature
Minneapolis-St. Paul:
 12°F (-11°C)
International Falls:
 2°F (-16°C)

Average July temperature
Minneapolis-St. Paul:
 72°F (22°C)
International Falls:
 66°F (19°C)

Average yearly rainfall
Minneapolis-St. Paul:
 26 inches (66 cm)
International Falls:
 26 inches (66 cm)

Average yearly snowfall
Minneapolis-St. Paul:
 46 inches (117 cm)
International Falls:
 60 inches (152 cm)

Major Rivers

Mississippi River
2,340 miles (3,765 km)

Red River of the North
545 miles (877 km)

Minnesota River
332 miles (534 km)

St. Croix River
164 miles (264 km)

L. of the Woods
Rainy R.
Agassiz Pool
Kabetogama L.
Voyageurs NP
Upper Red L.
Pelican L.
Trout L.
Grand Portage NM
Lower Red L.
Vermilion L.
Eagle Mt.
L. Winnibigoshish
Vermilion Range
Birch L.
Cass L.
Mesabi Range
Lake Superior
L. Itasca
Mississippi R.
Leech L.
Fish L. Res.
Island L. Res.
Outer I.
Stockton I.
Cuyuna Range
Big Sandy L.
Madeline I.
Otter Tail L.
Gull L.
Mille Lacs L.
Saint Croix NSR
L. Osakis
L. Traverse
Mississippi R.
Big Stone L.
L. Minnewaska
St. Croix R.
Mississippi NRA
St. Anthonys Falls
Minnesota R.
Mississippi R.
Des Moines R.
L. Hanska
Pipestone NM

SCALE/KEY

| 0 | 50 Miles |
| 0 | 50 Kilometers |

NM	National Monument
NP	National Park
NRA	National Resource Area
NSR	National Scenic River
▲	Highest Point
	Mountains

Hills, Valleys, and Prairies

Not surprisingly for a state with a large land area, Minnesota encompasses a variety of geographical features. The southern half of the state is hilly, with valleys formed by the many rivers. In the northeast the hills become almost mountainous, while the northwest contains prairies and marshes. The northern and eastern parts of the state are largely forested, with evergreens to the north and deciduous trees to the south. Since lumber has been a major industry in the state since the mid-nineteenth century, relatively little of Minnesota's old-growth evergreen forest remains.

Plants and Animals

Minnesota flora is divided roughly into three types: evergreen forest in the northeast, deciduous forest in the south, and prairie in the south and west. Among the native coniferous trees are pine, spruce, fir, and tamarack. Wildflowers of Minnesota include dutchman's breeches, bloodroot, and fairy slipper. Prairie lilies, coneflowers, and pasture roses brighten the prairies of the state in the summer. Wildlife is abundant in Minnesota, ranging from black bears, moose, wolves, lynx, and bobcats to deer, raccoons, woodchucks, porcupines, and gophers. The earliest Europeans to visit the area were trappers and hunters, and many of the species they pursued are still present throughout the state. Of course the "land of 10,000 lakes" is also a fisher's paradise. Common game fish in Minnesota include walleye, northern pike, bass, whitefish, and rainbow trout.

Largest Lakes

Upper Red Lake
288,800 acres
(116,877 hectares)

Mille Lacs Lake
132,516 acres
(53,629 ha)

Leech Lake
111, 527 acres
(45,135 ha)

Lake Winnibigoshish
58,544 acres
(23,693 ha)

▼ White-tailed deer are plentiful in Minnesota's woodlands.

From Timber to High-Tech

> The indications, from geological surveys of Minnesota, do not favor the hopes of great metallic wealth within its borders.
>
> — *from* The New World in 1859, Being the United States and Canada, Illustrated and Described

One of Minnesota's earliest commodities was pipestone, a unique red rock Native Americans used to make peace pipes. They traveled from as far as 1,000 miles (1,609 km) away to mine the quarries in the southern part of the state. The quarries still function today within the confines of Pipestone National Monument.

Minnesota's abundant wildlife first brought trappers and traders to the region. Then timber became the state's most important resource. Iron ore was soon to follow with the discovery of the Mesabi Range in 1884. Both of these resources have had an enormous impact on the economy and the environment of the state.

Transportation

Minnesota's rivers and streams have provided a critical link to the east, south, and north. With access via the Mississippi River to the Gulf of Mexico; via the Great Lakes and St. Lawrence River to the northern Atlantic Coast; and via the Red River of the North to Hudson Bay in Canada, goods — and people — could be moved virtually anywhere. From the first trappers and hunters who exported pelts and other animal products, to the farmers shipping grain, to the massive traffic of timber from the logging industry, Minnesota's waterways have played a critical part in practically every historical economic development.

Today the Twin Cities are the state's transportation hub. Most products being exported from the state move through the Twin Cities, often on their way to Duluth, the busiest port on the Great Lakes. The Minneapolis-St. Paul

Top Employers (of workers age sixteen and over)	
Services	29.6%
Wholesale and retail trade	23.7%
Manufacturing	16.1%
Finance, insurance, and real estate	6.7%
Transportation, communications, and other public utilities	6.6%
Construction	5.0%
Agriculture, forestry, and fisheries	4.2%
Public Administration	3.2%
Mining	0.4%

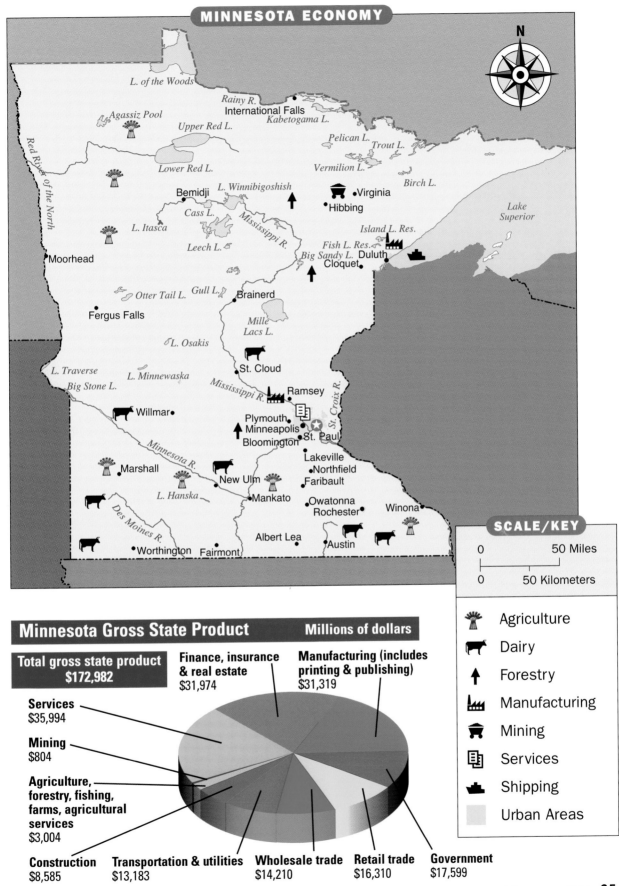

MINNESOTA ECONOMY

N

L. of the Woods
Rainy R.
International Falls
Kabetogama L.
Agassiz Pool
Upper Red L.
Pelican L.
Trout L.
Red River of the North
Lower Red L.
Vermilion L.
Birch L.
Bemidji
L. Winnibigoshish
Virginia
Cass L.
Hibbing
Lake Superior
L. Itasca
Mississippi R.
Island L. Res.
Fish L. Res.
Moorhead
Leech L.
Big Sandy L.
Duluth
Cloquet
Otter Tail L.
Gull L.
Brainerd
Fergus Falls
Mille Lacs L.
L. Osakis
St. Cloud
L. Traverse
L. Minnewaska
Mississippi R.
Ramsey
Big Stone L.
Willmar
Plymouth
Minneapolis
St. Paul
St. Croix R.
Minnesota R.
Bloomington
Lakeville
Marshall
Northfield
New Ulm
Faribault
L. Hanska
Mankato
Owatonna
Rochester
Winona
Des Moines R.
Albert Lea
Austin
Worthington
Fairmont

SCALE/KEY

0 — 50 Miles
0 — 50 Kilometers

🌾 Agriculture
🐂 Dairy
↑ Forestry
🏭 Manufacturing
⛏ Mining
🗒 Services
⚓ Shipping
▨ Urban Areas

Minnesota Gross State Product

Millions of dollars

Total gross state product $172,982

Finance, insurance & real estate $31,974

Manufacturing (includes printing & publishing) $31,319

Services $35,994

Mining $804

Agriculture, forestry, fishing, farms, agricultural services $3,004

Construction $8,585

Transportation & utilities $13,183

Wholesale trade $14,210

Retail trade $16,310

Government $17,599

International Airport is a hub as well, bringing millions of travelers through the area on their way to destinations around the world.

Timber and Mining

Hundreds of years ago lumber was cut by clear-cutting acres of forest, leaving nothing behind. This technique reduced Minnesota's native evergreen forests drastically. Today environmental laws prevent clear-cutting. Modern efforts have reforested large portions of the state.

The region south of Lake Superior is rich in iron ore deposits, extending from Michigan through Wisconsin and into Minnesota. Iron mining began in Minnesota in the 1890s on the Vermilion, Mesabi, and Cuyuna Ranges.

Until recently iron ore mining has been one of the most important industries in Minnesota. The Mesabi Range alone produces three-quarters of the nation's iron ore. Like logging, mining is an industry that lasts only until its resources are exhausted. In the case of Minnesota's iron mines, this occurred to a great extent after World War II, when the last of the high-grade iron ore was removed from the earth. When the supply of high-grade ore from the state's three ranges diminished, a method was developed at the University of Minnesota to make the mining of taconite, the low-grade iron ore, profitable. Although sand, granite, and gravel have not been critical to the state's economy, Minnesota is among the nation's leading producers of these minerals.

▼ Although lumber (*inset*) is still an important industry, mining no longer plays a critical role in Minnesota's economy. Buildings of the former Mesabi Iron Company (*bottom*).

Agriculture

Agriculture is no longer a major employer in Minnesota, but it is still one of the largest industries. This is possible because mechanization and modern farming practices allow for efficient production with minimal labor. Corn and soybeans are grown in the southern part of the state. In the northwest, with its colder temperatures and shorter growing season, the main crops are wheat, barley, sugar beets, sunflowers, potatoes, and flax. In the wooded regions of the state, there are dairy farms.

▲ Harvesting wheat in the northwestern part of the state.

Manufacturing

Since World War II, manufacturing has experienced a steep rise in importance as part of the state's economy. As the lumber and mining industries decreased in importance, other higher-technology industries took their place. The technology and transportation company Honeywell has its roots in 1886 Minneapolis. Today the largest companies in Minnesota include 3M (Minnesota Mining and Manufacturing), the makers of Scotch tape and Post-it Notes; General Mills, which makes food products; and Medtronic Inc., a medical device company. Lumber has once again become an important industry. Pines and other trees are harvested for making pulp (for paper products) and aspens are harvested for making waferboard.

Made in Minnesota

Leading farm products and crops
Wheat
Corn
Soybeans
Dairy products

Other products
Machinery
Food products
Electrical equipment
Forest products

Trade and Finance

Like the service sector, trade and finance have become critical to Minnesota's economy. The chain stores Target and Best Buy have their corporate headquarters in Minnesota, and more important, nearly a quarter of the state's workers are employed in wholesale or retail trade. Banks and insurance companies are among the state's largest companies as well.

Major Airport		
Airport	Location	Passengers per year (2001)
Minneapolis/ St. Paul International	Minneapolis/St. Paul	36,751,632

Third Party's the Charm

The state must reaffirm its commitment to quality service for its citizens, with success measured by actual outcomes rather than process, and to a cost-conscious state government.

— *Gov. Jesse Ventura, October 1999*

I n 1837 Colonel Henry Dodge signed a treaty with the Anishinabe people whereby they relinquished much of their land east of the Mississippi. The next year the Dakota signed a treaty giving up their lands west of the Mississippi. The stage was set for Minnesota to become a territory of its own. This happened twelve years later, as settlers began to pour into the region.

The drive toward statehood was happening at the same time that the political landscape of the United States was changing. The Whig party, one of the nation's original political parties, was dying out. The Democratic party was by far the largest and most powerful in the country, but many people were dissatisfied with the Democrats' tolerance of slavery. In response, the Republican party was founded in 1854 and quickly grew to a position of national prominence.

The rise of the Republican party and the ideals for which it stood were important to the people of Minnesota. Although the state's most established population, in the timber country of the northeast, tended to support the Democratic party, the settlers who were quickly occupying the southern and western plains and hills favored personal freedom and opposed slavery. The new party appealed to them.

The territory's first governor in 1849, Alexander Ramsey, was a Whig. In 1853 the Democrats gained control of the territorial government. Although there were difficulties at the state's constitutional convention in 1857 because of an even split between Democratic and Republican delegates, the two parties' representatives produced two nearly identical constitutions. When the differences were hammered out and

State Constitution

The stability of a republican form of government depending mainly upon the intelligence of the people, it shall be the duty of the legislature to establish a general and uniform system of public schools.

— *from the Minnesota State Constitution, 1857*

the document put to a vote of the people, it passed almost unanimously. Minnesota was admitted to the Union on May 11, 1858, becoming the thirty-second state.

State Government

Jesse Ventura, the first third-party — neither Democratic nor Republican — governor elected in Minnesota since 1936, was a member of the Reform party when he was elected in 1998. He later left the party due to differences over the direction the national party was taking. He is affiliated with the Independence party of Minnesota, making him the only governor in the United States not affiliated with a major party.

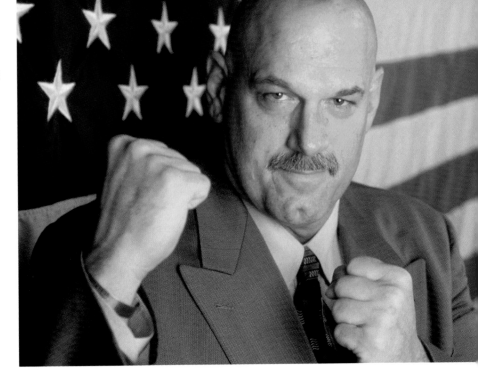

▲ Minnesota governor Jesse Ventura was a professional wrestler before entering politics.

The Executive Branch

The state constitution defines six elected officials in the executive branch. The governor is the head of state, responsible for enforcing state laws and providing leadership to the entire state. The lieutenant governor assists and advises the governor and is prepared to take the governor's place if an emergency should arise. The state auditor oversees the finances of the state and local governments. The attorney general is the chief legal officer

Elected Posts in the Executive Branch		
Office	Length of Term	Term Limits
Governor	4 years	2 consecutive terms
Lieutenant Governor	4 years	None
State Auditor	4 years	None
Attorney General	4 years	None
State Treasurer	4 years	None
Secretary of State	4 years	None

of the state. The treasurer safeguards and oversees state funds. The secretary of state administers and oversees state functions, such as elections and business services.

In addition to the six elected officials, the executive branch of the state government includes many departments and agencies, such as the Department of Human Services, the Pollution Control Agency, and the Department of Corrections.

The Legislative Branch

The Minnesota State Legislature has two branches, the senate and the house of representatives. There are two representatives and one senator for each of the state's sixty-seven legislative districts, for a total of 201 members of the Legislature. The speaker of the house and the president of the senate are elected by the members of each house on the first day of each session. A new session begins every other year. Redistricting (rearranging the legislative districts) occurs after each U.S. Census to reflect changes in the population of each district.

Sessions last from January of each odd-numbered year to May of the next year. The actual dates on which the Legislature may meet are the first Tuesday after the first Monday in January until the first Monday following the third Saturday in May of the same year. The Legislature may meet for a total of 120 days during each session. In practice daily sessions usually take place between January and May of odd-numbered years and between February and April of even-numbered years. The governor may call a special session, but the length and purpose of special sessions are decided by the Legislature.

The Judicial Branch

The Minnesota court system has three levels: trial court, the court of appeals, and the supreme court. The 241 district court and 16 appellate court justices are appointed

State Legislature			
House	Number of Members	Length of Term	Term Limits
Senate	67 senators	4 years*	None
House of Representatives	134 representatives	2 years	None

* Senators elected in years ending in "0," such as 2000, serve two-year terms. This allows redistricting to take effect immediately after the U.S. Census is completed.

by the governor, but they must be reelected by the people after their first terms are up. Terms last six years. Cases are heard in the trial courts. The court of appeals does not hold trials, but hears and reviews cases to determine whether a trial was fair and rules were followed.

Cases that are still in dispute after a review at the appellate level may be submitted to the supreme court. The cases heard by the supreme court are usually selected because they will set precedents or affect how the state constitution is interpreted. In addition to hearing appeals, the supreme court is responsible for overseeing the entire state judicial system. The justices are responsible for supervising the court system and overseeing the practice of law in Minnesota.

There are currently seven justices on the supreme court, but, when it was established in the Minnesota Territory in 1849, there were only three. Justices are elected to six-year terms. If a justice leaves office for any reason during a term, the governor will appoint a new justice to replace him or her.

Pact for Peace

In 1929 U.S. Secretary of State Frank B. Kellogg, a Minnesotan, was awarded the Nobel Peace Prize for his work on the Kellogg-Briand Peace Pact. The pact, signed by the United States, Germany, France, and the United Kingdom, renounced war as an instrument of foreign policy.

▼ World-renowned architect Cass Gilbert designed the state capitol in St. Paul. He also designed New York City's Woolworth building.

Water, Water Everywhere

> In St. Paul and Minneapolis one thing notable is the cordial hospitality, another is the public spirit, and another is the intense devotion to business, the forecast and alertness in new enterprises.
>
> — *Charles Dudley Warner*, Studies in the South and West, *1889*

In a state with over fifteen thousand lakes and 92,000 miles (148,028 km) of rivers, it is hardly surprising that the most popular pastimes would be water-based. Boating is a favorite activity, from canoeing to sailing to yachting. Waterskiing also has a big following. Minnesotan Ralph Samuelson invented the sport in 1922.

Minnesota sells more fishing licenses per capita than any other state in the nation. It is estimated that 2.3 million people — or nearly half the state's population — go fishing every year. Among the fish common in the state are walleye, trout, and bass. Despite the fact that Minnesota has some of the harshest winters in the nation, the fishing doesn't stop when the leaves fall off the trees. Ice fishing goes on throughout the coldest months. Enthusiasts build "fish houses" on the frozen lakes. The tiny houses are warm inside, and a hole cut through the ice gives access to the water beneath.

Outstate and the Cities

In many ways the Twin Cities define Minnesota's personality. In fact, they are so important that everyone outside the metropolitan area just calls them "the Cities." And to the city folk, everyone else is "outstate."

◀ Waterskiing was invented in 1922 in Minnesota, and the sport remains popular there.

Winter Sports

A state famous for its winters has to have an abundance of cold-weather sports. Hockey is one of the most popular, and the state has produced a number of National Hockey League (NHL) players. Ice-skating, snowmobiling, and cross-country skiing are all well-represented among the state's activities. In fact, Minnesota has more than 2,000 miles (3,218 km) of snowmobile trails and was home to one of the first commercial snowmobile manufacturers. Cross-country skiing enthusiasts also can make use of miles of ski trails.

▲ Duluth residents kayak on Lake Superior *(top)*. Minnesota winters provide ample opportunity to enjoy winter sports such as snowmobiling *(inset)*.

Literary Links

Minnesota has been home to a number of famous writers, including novelists, humorists, and poets. F. Scott Fitzgerald, author of *The Great Gatsby* (1925) and other works, was born in St. Paul in 1896. One of the most celebrated U.S. authors, he wrote his first novel while living in St. Paul.

Sinclair Lewis hailed from Sauk Centre, where he lived from his birth in 1885 until he left for college in 1903. His satirical novel *Main Street* (1920) was based on life in his hometown. Lewis became the first American to win the Nobel Prize for literature, in 1930.

Garrison Keillor might be the person best known for his association with Minnesota. Born in Anoka in 1942, Keillor came to prominence as the host of the radio program "A Prairie Home Companion," a variety show that features folk music, comedy, and Keillor's original stories about life in his imaginary hometown of Lake Wobegon. His portrayal, both on the radio and in short stories and novels, of the community of "Norwegian bachelor farmers" with its combination of small-town simplicity and moral sophistication, is for many the epitome of the Minnesota spirit.

Although not born in the state, Laura Ingalls Wilder had an important connection to Minnesota. The author of the *Little House on the Prairie* series of books drew heavily on her experiences as a homesteader in the nineteenth century. Wilder lived in Minnesota several times between 1874 and 1890. Her first home in Minnesota was on Plum Creek, near present-day Walnut Grove, where she moved with her family when she was seven years old. Today the town features the Wilder Museum, which exhibits memorabilia from the television series based on her books, and the Ingalls Homestead, where the lands described in *On the Banks of Plum Creek* (1937) are still preserved.

Poet Robert Bly was born in Madison in 1926. He grew up in the state, attending St. Olaf College before going on to Harvard for graduate school. A recipient of numerous prestigious fellowships and grants, Bly won the National Book Award in poetry in 1968 for *The Light Around the Body* (1967).

Science fiction writer Clifford D. Simak, born in Millville, Wisconsin, in 1904, moved to Minnesota in the 1930s and began working for the *Minneapolis Star* and *The Tribune*. He continued to work as a writer and editor until 1976, while at the same time becoming one of the most celebrated science fiction authors in the country. Among the major awards he received were the Hugo Award and the International Fantasy Award. Simak died in Minneapolis in 1988.

Minnesota Original

Garrison Keillor hosts Minnesota's best-known radio show, "A Prairie Home Companion." First produced in 1974, it is now broadcast on more than 511 public radio stations.

Sport	Team	Home
Baseball	Minnesota Twins	Metrodome, Minneapolis
Basketball	Minnesota Timberwolves	Target Center, Minneapolis
	Minnesota Lynx (WNBA)	Target Center, Minneapolis
Football	Minnesota Vikings	Metrodome, Minneapolis
Hockey	Minnesota Wild	Xcel Energy Center, St. Paul

Sports

Minnesota is well-represented in major sports at the professional and collegiate level. The University of Minnesota Golden Gophers, members of the Big Ten conference, regularly field nationally-ranked teams in football as well as men's and women's basketball. The Twin Cities are home to many major professional sports teams. The Twins won the World Series in 1987 and again in 1991. The Timberwolves are one of the National Basketball Association's (NBA's) newest teams, having joined the league in 1989. They reached the playoffs for the first time in the 1996–1997 season. When the North Stars left Bloomington in 1993 (to become the Dallas Stars), thousands of hockey fans across Minnesota were devastated. The newest team in town, however, is the Minnesota Wild, which began play in the National Hockey League (NHL) in the 2000–2001 season.

The Arts

The Twin Cities are rich in theaters that cater to audiences of all ages. Major venues include the Guthrie Theater, one of the most respected theaters in the world; the Children's Theater Company; and In the Heart of the Beast Puppet and Mask Theater. From the traditional to the modern,

▶ The Minnesota Wild played its first season in 2000–2001.

Minneapolis Lakers

Did you ever wonder why the Los Angeles basketball team is called the Lakers? It's because the team started out in Minnesota, the Land of 10,000 Lakes. The Minneapolis Lakers won five NBA titles between 1949 and 1954. Only a few years later, the team fell to the bottom of the league. The Lakers moved to Los Angeles after a disappointing 1960 season.

there are troupes devoted to performing dramas, comedies, dance, musicals, and everything in between.

For those who find music more appealing than theater, Minnesota has plenty to offer. Classical music is well-represented by the Minnesota Orchestra and the Minnesota Opera, both located in Minneapolis, as well as the St. Paul Chamber Orchestra. On the lighter side, Minneapolis is also home to the Gilbert and Sullivan Very Light Opera Company. And don't forget rock and roll! Minneapolis is home to the artist once again known as Prince.

Museums

Before taking in a live theater performance, visitors can spend the day enjoying some of Minnesota's many museums. The Walker Art Center in Minneapolis is a world-famous museum of U.S. and European contemporary art. Adjacent to the Walker Art Center is the Minneapolis Sculpture Garden, the largest sculpture park in any U.S. city. Visitors can wander among trees, flower beds, and works by artists such as Louise Bourgeois, Mark di Suvero, and architect Frank Gehry. Some of the Twin Cities' other art museums include the Minnesota Museum of American Art in St. Paul; the

◀ Two popular St. Paul destinations are *(left)* the Science Museum of Minnesota and *(inset)* the Ordway Center for the Performing Arts.

Frederick R. Weisman Art Museum at the University of Minnesota; and the Minnesota Children's Museum in St. Paul. Other places of note are the Science Museum of Minnesota in St. Paul, which houses the largest collection of "questionable" medical devices on display in the United States, and the Lake Superior Railroad Museum in Duluth. The Mille Lacs Indian Museum in Onamia explores and celebrates the culture and history of the Mille Lacs band of Ojibwa.

▲ The Spoonbridge and Cherry sculpture, by Claes Oldenburg and Coosje van Bruggen, is the centerpiece of the Minneapolis Sculpture Garden.

Attractions

For shoppers the place to go is the Mall of America in Bloomington. The largest indoor mall in the United States, it opened in 1992. It now houses more than five hundred stores, a 7-acre (3-ha) amusement park, and an aquarium. The mall is among the most-visited U.S. tourist attractions. More than forty million people visit each year. It is estimated that 40 percent of the mall's visitors come from more than 150 miles (241 km) away.

The Valleyfair Amusement Park in Shakopee is the largest amusement park in the Midwest. It features 90 acres (36 ha) of rides and amusements, including a water park. Paul Bunyan's Animal Land in Bemidji is an animal park featuring many exotic species. Visitors can get up close and personal with lions, tigers, tortoises, and dozens of other animals. Minnesota is also home to many zoos, including the Minnesota Zoo in Apple Valley, the Como Zoo and Conservatory in St. Paul, and the Lake Superior Zoo in Duluth.

Stars of the North

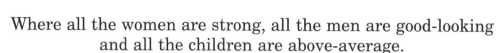

> Where all the women are strong, all the men are good-looking and all the children are above-average.
>
> — *Garrison Keillor describing the fictional Lake Wobegon on "A Prairie Home Companion," 1987*

Following are only a few of the thousands of people who were born, died, or spent much of their lives in Minnesota and made extraordinary contributions to the state and the nation.

THE MAYO BROTHERS
SURGEONS
WILLIAM JAMES MAYO
BORN: *June 29, 1861, Le Sueur*
DIED: *July 28, 1939, Rochester*

CHARLES HORACE MAYO
BORN: *July 19, 1865, Rochester*
DIED: *May 26, 1939, Chicago, IL*

In 1888, after the Mayo brothers had each earned their medical degrees, they entered private practice with their father. In 1889 they formed a cooperative group clinic in Rochester. William Mayo was the hospital's administrator and Charles Mayo, one of the most brilliant surgeons in the country, created and refined new surgical techniques. The Mayo Clinic grew quickly because interns and researchers were attracted to the cooperative atmosphere. Today the Mayo Clinic is one of the world's premiere medical facilities.

ROY WILKINS
CIVIL RIGHTS LEADER
BORN: *August 30, 1901, St. Louis, MO*
DIED: *September 8, 1981, New York, NY*

Roy Wilkins once said that he believed there were "more people who want to do good than evil" in the world. Working from this belief, Wilkins dedicated his life to securing civil rights for African Americans. Wilkins was raised in St. Paul and attended the University of Minnesota. While in college he joined the National Association for the Advancement of Colored People (NAACP), an organization he would one day lead. After college, Wilkins was a writer for the *Kansas City Call*, an African-American newspaper in Missouri. In 1931 he became the NAACP's assistant executive secretary. Wilkins investigated claims of discrimination and protested unfair treatment as well as editing *Crisis*, the NAACP's magazine. In 1955 he was made the NAACP's executive secretary and led the group through the most significant period in its history. As spokesman Wilkins testified before many congressional hearings and consulted with presidents. One of the greatest moments in his illustrious career was the 1963 March on Washington, which he helped organize and at which he spoke. Wilkins remained head of the NAACP until he retired in 1977.

CHARLES LINDBERGH
AVIATOR

BORN: *February 4, 1902, Detroit, MI*
DIED: *August 26, 1974, Maui, HI*

Famous aviator Charles Augustus Lindbergh grew up in Little Falls, Minnesota. Lindbergh dropped out of college in his second year and enrolled in flight school. He bought a World War I Curtiss Jenny, became a stunt pilot for a time, attended Army flight school, and then became an air mail pilot. His most famous exploit came as the result of a contest to cross the Atlantic Ocean by air. With a group of financial backers and a team of engineers, Lindbergh designed and built the *Spirit of St. Louis*. In 1927 he successfully made the first nonstop transatlantic flight in thirty-three and one-half hours. He took off from New York on May 20 and arrived, to be mobbed by a crowd of admirers, in Paris on May 21. Later in 1927 the U.S. Congress awarded him the Medal of Honor.

HUBERT HUMPHREY
STATESMAN

BORN: *May 27, 1911, Wallace, SD*
DIED: *January 13, 1978, Waverly*

A South Dakota native, Hubert Horatio Humphrey graduated from the University of Minnesota. He was elected U.S. Senator from Minnesota in 1948. Humphrey, a Democrat, was an outspoken proponent of civil rights and was known as one of the most liberal members of the Senate. In 1964 he was elected as Lyndon B. Johnson's vice president. Although Humphrey drew criticism for supporting the war in Vietnam, he continued to be a champion of civil rights and other liberal causes. He was nominated to run for U.S. president by the Democratic party in 1968 but lost a close election to Richard M. Nixon. In 1970 he was reelected to the U.S. Senate and served until his death.

JUDY GARLAND
ACTRESS

BORN: *June 10, 1922, Grand Rapids*
DIED: *June 22, 1969, London, England*

Born Frances Gumm to a family of vaudeville performers, Judy Garland made her stage debut at the age of three. A talented singer and actress, she made a series of successful films starring opposite Mickey Rooney. Garland is best known for her role as Dorothy in *The Wizard of Oz*, for which she won an honorary Oscar award. Although she continued to star in hit movies and remained a popular actress, Garland had drug problems and was eventually fired by MGM in 1950 for continually showing up late to work. Her popularity never waned, but her screen career never fully recovered. She died of an overdose of sleeping pills.

CHARLES SCHULZ
CARTOONIST

BORN: *November 26, 1922, Minneapolis*
DIED: *February 12, 2000, Santa Rosa, CA*

The creator of the comic strip "Peanuts" was born and raised in Minneapolis. After graduating from high school, he began drawing. He produced cartoons for the *St. Paul Pioneer Press* and the *Saturday Evening Post* in the 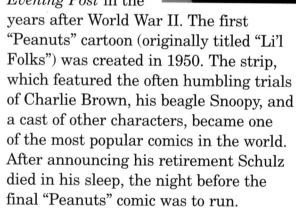 years after World War II. The first "Peanuts" cartoon (originally titled "Li'l Folks") was created in 1950. The strip, which featured the often humbling trials of Charlie Brown, his beagle Snoopy, and a cast of other characters, became one of the most popular comics in the world. After announcing his retirement Schulz died in his sleep, the night before the final "Peanuts" comic was to run.

WALTER MONDALE
STATESMAN

BORN: *January 5, 1928, Ceylon, MN*

A lifelong Minnesotan, Walter Frederick Mondale got his political start when he managed Hubert Humphrey's campaign for the U.S. Senate in 1948. While practicing law in Minneapolis, he managed the reelection campaign of Democratic governor Orville Freeman. The governor appointed Mondale state attorney general in 1960, and he was elected for two terms thereafter. After Humphrey was elected vice president in 1964, Mondale was appointed to fill Humphrey's seat in the Senate and then was elected to the post for two successive terms. In 1976 Mondale was himself elected vice president, running on the Democratic ticket with Jimmy Carter. In 1984 Mondale received the Democratic nomination for president and selected as his running mate Geraldine Ferraro, the first woman on the presidential ticket of a major political party. The Mondale-Ferraro team lost in a landslide reelection of Ronald Reagan. One of the few states they carried was Minnesota.

BOB DYLAN
MUSICIAN

BORN: *May 24, 1941, Duluth, Minnesota*

In 1959 Robert Allen Zimmerman adopted his more famous surname as a tribute to the poet Dylan Thomas. Raised in the mining town of Hibbing, Dylan began playing rock and roll and folk music as a teenager. He was a member of the Greenwich Village, New York, folk music scene in the early 1960s, producing records that quickly earned him critical acclaim and national popularity. One of the leading figures in folk music throughout the 1960s, he soon began adding electric instruments to his recordings and became an idol to millions of rock and roll fans. Dylan continues to be a popular performer today. In 1988 he was inducted into the Rock and Roll Hall of Fame, and in 1998 he won three Grammy Awards, including album of the year for *Time Out of Mind*.

JESSE VENTURA
GOVERNOR

BORN: *July 15, 1951, Minneapolis*

After graduating from high school in Minneapolis, Jesse George Janos joined the U.S. Navy and served in the Vietnam War. When he returned home, he worked briefly as a bouncer at a nightclub in Brooklyn Park. In 1973 Janos changed his name to Ventura and began his career as a professional wrestler known as "The Body." After eleven years Ventura left the ring and became an actor and wrestling commentator. In 1990 he ran for mayor of Brooklyn Park and won, serving until 1995. After his term as mayor, Ventura was a radio DJ for several years. In 1998 he ran for governor of the state as the candidate of the Reform party, and to the surprise of many, he won. Ventura is known for being outspoken and unconventional. He is the first Reform party candidate ever to have won a statewide office.

ANN BANCROFT
EXPLORER AND TEACHER

BORN: *September 29, 1955, St. Paul*

The first woman to reach both the North and South Poles, Ann Bancroft grew up camping, canoeing, and adventuring in Minnesota's wilderness. Coming from a courageous family, it was natural for Bancroft to drop everything to join the Steger International North Pole Expedition, which in 1986 reached the North Pole via dogsled. She has also skied across Greenland and led three other women on a sixty-seven-day skiing trip across Antarctica to the South Pole. She was honored as *Ms.* magazine's Woman of the Year in 1987, and her exploits have earned her a place in the National Women's Hall of Fame.

PRINCE
MUSICIAN

BORN: *June 7, 1958, Minneapolis*

From Prince Rogers Nelson's earliest days, he showed a prodigious musical talent. He was equally adept at drums, guitar, and keyboards, and when he signed his first record deal in 1978, he insisted on being given complete creative control over the record. Although this was an unprecedented demand, Warner Bros. reluctantly agreed to it, and the legend of Prince was born. His music has run the gamut from rock to soul to jazz, and he has emerged as one of the most popular performers in the world. After taking a hiatus from the music world for several years (and temporarily dropping his name, becoming known as "the artist formerly known as Prince"), he has returned for the new millennium.

Minnesota

History At-A-Glance

1659
French explorers Radisson and Groseilliers begin to explore the region.

1673
Jolliet and Marquette explore the upper Mississippi River.

1680
Father Louis Hennepin, while being held captive by a group of Dakota, becomes the first European to see St. Anthony Falls.

1695
Le Sueur establishes a trading post on Prairie Island in the Mississippi River.

1763
The Treaty of Paris transfers eastern Minnesota from French to British control.

1783
The Revolutionary War ends, transfers British control of eastern Minnesota to the United States.

1803
The Louisiana Purchase brings Minnesota west of the Mississippi under U.S. control.

1818
Michigan Territory is extended to include the eastern half of Minnesota.

1832
Henry Schoolcraft locates the source of the Mississippi River in north-central Minnesota.

1849
Minnesota Territory established.

1858
Minnesota admitted to the Union as the thirty-second state.

1861
Minnesota is the first state to volunteer troops to defend the Union in the Civil War.

1600   **1700**   **1800**

1492
Christopher Columbus comes to New World.

1607
Capt. John Smith and three ships land on Virginia coast and start first English settlement in New World — Jamestown.

1754–63
French and Indian War.

1773
Boston Tea Party.

1776
Declaration of Independence adopted July 4.

1777
Articles of Confederation adopted by Continental Congress.

1787
U.S. Constitution written.

1812–14
War of 1812.

United States

History At-A-Glance

1862
The Dakota conflict breaks out, ultimately leaving more than four hundred dead.

1889
The Mayo Clinic opens as St. Marys Hospital in Rochester.

1905
Construction is completed on the third (and current) state capitol, in St. Paul.

1912
The first Better Business Bureau in United States opens in Minneapolis.

1932
More goods produced in Minnesota factories than on state farms.

1937
Pipestone National Monument is created, protecting the Native American pipestone quarries.

1951
Minnesota produces 82 percent of the nation's iron ore.

1964
Hubert Humphrey becomes the first Minnesotan elected vice president.

1976
Walter Mondale becomes the second Minnesotan elected vice president.

1987
The Minnesota Twins win the World Series for the first time. They will win again in 1991.

1990
The Minnesota Supreme Court becomes the first state supreme court to have a majority of women justices.

1998
Reform party candidate Jesse Ventura is elected governor, the first third-party governor since 1936.

1800   **1900**   **2000**

1848
Gold discovered in California draws eighty thousand prospectors in the 1849 Gold Rush.

1861–65
Civil War.

1869
Transcontinental railroad completed.

1917–18
U.S. involvement in World War I.

1929
Stock market crash ushers in Great Depression.

1941–45
U.S. involvement in World War II.

1950–53
U.S. fights in the Korean War.

1964–73
U.S. involvement in Vietnam War.

2000
George W. Bush wins the closest presidential election in history.

2001
A terrorist attack in which four hijacked airliners crash into New York City's World Trade Center, the Pentagon, and farmland in western Pennsylvania leaves thousands dead or injured.

▼ The Red Jacket Concrete Bridge near Mankato was opened to the public in 1911.

Festivals and Fun for All

Check web site for exact date and directions.

East Central Minnesota Sheep and Wool Festival, **Mora**

Sheep-shearing, spinning demonstrations, and more.
www.rogerhislop.com/sheep

Festival of Adventures, **Aitkin**

A celebration of the early historical period of the fur trade and steamboating. Features living-history interpreters and exhibits.
www.aitkin.com/fest

Fiddlers Festival, Minnesota Pioneer Park, **Annandale**

Pioneer Park is a living-history park with demonstrations of pioneer life. The annual fiddling competition also features clog dancing.
www.pioneerpark.org/events.html

Heritagefest, **New Ulm**

An annual celebration of German heritage, this has been named one of the top one hundred festivals in North America.
www.heritagefest.net

Lumberjack Days Festival, **Stillwater**

Lumberjack shows, concerts, contests, road races, pancake breakfasts, and parades make this festival fun for all.
www.lumberjackdays.com

Minnesota Bluegrass and Old-Time Music Association Festival, **El Rancho Mañana**

This three-day festival of acoustic music in rural Minnesota is one of the largest bluegrass festivals in the Upper Midwest. It features a campsite for those who don't want to leave, as well as shows, workshops, and dancing.
www.minnesotabluegrass.org/events/mbotmf

The Minnesota Fringe Festival, **Minneapolis**

A live performance festival to promote free expression and diversity of artistic endeavors. The festival features theater, storytelling, puppetry, traditional crafts, food, and much more.
www.fringe festival.org

▶ A puppet created for the Minnesota Fringe Festival.

Minnesota Irish Fair, St. Paul

A celebration of Irish heritage, featuring puppets and storytelling, sheepherding demonstrations, and more.

www.irishfair.com

Minnesota Renaissance Festival, Shakopee

If you have a suit of armor you've been waiting for the right occasion to wear, you can finally break it in. The festival runs weekends from mid-August through the end of September, and many different events with wide-ranging cultures take place — from the Middle East to Italy to Scotland.

www.renaissancefest.com/minnesota-main.htm

Minnesota Shakespeare Festival, Grand Marais

This two-week event features a variety of activities, from cooking and swing dance classes to tea and scones, and of course, performances of Shakespeare's plays.

www.grandmaraisplayhouse.com

Minnesota State Fair, midway between St. Paul and Minneapolis

First held in 1859, this agricultural fair has grown to include entertainment, industrial and technological exhibits, rides, and everything else you would expect to find at a state fair.

www.mnstatefair.org

Nisswa-Stämman Scandinavian Folk Music Festival, Nisswa

A celebration of Scandinavian folk music. Two days of concerts, children's events, folk dancing, and a smorgasbord as well as an *allspel*, when all the artists from all the different acts play together.

www.brainerd.net/~pwilson/nisswastamman

St. Paul Winter Carnival, St. Paul

This winter celebration began in 1886. Today it features a giant snow slide, curling, ice sculptures, ice carving, winter-themed sports, shows, parades, and more.

www.winter-carnival.com

► In curling, team players sweep the ice to help the "rock" along the path to the target.

Books

Budak, Michael. *Grand Mound*. St. Paul, MN: Minnesota Historical Society Press, 1995. Archaeologist Michael Budak reveals the meaning and importance of the mound located near International Falls.

Greenberg, Keith Elliot. *Jesse Ventura*. Minneapolis, MN: Lerner Publications, 1999. A biography of the pro-wrestler turned Minnesota governor.

Marsh, Carole. *Minnesota Government for Kids: The Cornerstone of Everyday Life in Our State!* Peachtree, GA: Gallopade International, 1999. The government and laws of Minnesota.

Marsh, Carole. *Minnesota Indians!: A Kid's Look at Our State's Chiefs, Tribes, Reservations, Powwows, Lore and More from the Past and the Present*. Peachtree, GA: Gallopade International, 1996. An overview of the Native Americans of Minnesota.

Murphy, Nora, and Mary Murphy-Gnatz. *African Americans in Minnesota: Telling Our Own Stories*. St. Paul, MN: Minnesota Historical Society Press, 2000. The lives of African Americans in Minnesota, from the 1800s through today.

Paulsen, Gary. *Soldier's Heart: Being the Story of the Enlistment and Due Service of the Boy Charley Goddard in the First Minnesota Volunteers*. New York, NY: Laurel Leaf Books, 1996. Acclaimed author Gary Paulsen writes a fictionalized account of the true story of Charley Goddard, a fifteen-year-old Civil War volunteer from Minnesota.

Web Sites

▶ Minnesota state web site
www.state.mn.us

▶ Minnesota Historical Society
www.mnhs.org

▶ International Wolf Center in Ely, Minnesota
www.wolf.org

Films

Berg, Kristian. *The Dakota Conflict*. St. Paul, Minnesota: KTCA-TV, 1992. A sixty-minute documentary detailing the causes and effects of the Dakota Uprising of 1862.

Note: Page numbers in *italics* refer to maps, illustrations, or photographs.